YOUNG WRITERS

ALL ABOARD FOR

POWYS AND GWENT

First published in Great Britain in 1996 by
POETRY NOW
1-2 Wainman Road, Woodston,
Peterborough, PE2 7BU

HB ISBN 1 85731 708 4
SB ISBN 1 85731 702 5

Foreword

Toot, Toot! All Aboard! Set sail on a fantastic journey through the minds of today's children. Along the way we hope you will be charmed and enlightened by the thoughts, feelings and humour expressed by these young writers.

The poems included in this anthology have been selected for their exciting imagination, depth of feelings and down to earth language; revealing these children's awareness of various important issues close to many of our hearts. Now you can finally find out what these children *really* think of their parents, teachers and why trees lose their leaves in autumn!

We hope that you will sit back and enjoy this on-board entertainment, and we wish you a pleasant journey. Bon voyage!

CONTENTS

	Lee Simonds	76
	Rhys Elsworth	76
	Julie Crane	76
	Stephen North	77
	Nicola Barker	77
	Matthew Bissett	77
	Emma Turecek	78
	Dana Seaborne	78
	Samuel Williams	79
	Caroline Hughes	79
	Jennifer Hearne	79
	Natasha Turecek	80
	Laura Murphy	80
Langstone Primary School		
	Owen Burgess	81
	Bethan Coole	81
	Daniel Weston	82
	David Reece	82
	Lauren Masters	83
	Laura Cansfield	84
	Katie Farrands	85
	James Bowler	86
	Helen Price	87
	Kate Hobbs	88
	Lyndsey Parry	88
	Danielle Darbyshire	89
	James Johnston	90
	Aimée Pollard	90
	Susie Squire	91
	Jody Summers	92
Llantilio Pertholey School		
	Michael Hayward	93
	Gareth Edwards	93
	James Wham	94
	Daniel Morgan Maddock	94
	Matthew Worgan	94
	Bethan Williams	95
	Lewis Morgan	95

Kirsty Hicks	95
Jessica Collins	96
Matthew Bevan	96
Jade Perkins	96
Holly Williams	97
Rhys Davies	97
Peter Jay	97
Bethan Viveash	98
Lindsey Woodcock	98
Christopher Hill	99
Josh Wardle	99
Thomas Varley	100
Donna Norris	100
Stacey Bamber	101
Jonathan Ruck	101
Anthony Jones	102
Christopher Thomas	102
Ryan Jones	103
Abigail Thomas	103
Ellen Beaumont	104
Tom Birkett	104
Angus Macintosh	105
Lucy Niblett	105
Kelly Owen	106
Stefan Skinner	106

St Alban's RC Primary School, Pontypool

Elizabeth Taylor	107
Gemma Abramczyk	107
Ben Smith	108
Stephen Taylor	108
Emily Jordan-Patrikios	109
Matthew Dennehy	109
Joseph Gower	110
Jasmine Slingsby	110
Alexander Roberts	111
Jenna Lear	112
Carol Carey	113

St Gabriel's Primary School, Ringland		
	Danielle Watkins	114
	Natalie Moreland	114
	Sarah Nolan	115
	Marc Gunn	115
	Leon Trezise	116
	Esther Gush	116
	Katie Rudge	117
	Haley Fraser	117
	Nadia Llewellyn	118
	Amy Prothero	118
	Helen Corten	119
St Michael's School, Newport		
	Nicola Scarpato	119
	Karl Johansson	120
	Louis Yendle	121
Thornwell Primary School		
	Clare Hutchinson	122
	Hannah Sterry	122
	Louise Skidmore	123

THE SEASONS

In springtime when leaves are young,
Drops of water like jewels hung,
In between the leaves among.

In summer when birds leave the nest,
They hunt for worms and have a rest,
Back at their little nest.

In autumn when some waters freeze,
And naked trees sway in the breeze,
And swallows fly across the seas.

In winter when snow comes down,
Everyone has a great big frown,
So happy to see the snow,
Fluttering high then so low.

Now the year's begun again,
A boy says there is no snow then,
It is spring again with rain,
Splashing on the window pane.

It's summer, it's very hot,
I plant seeds in a pot,
Then they'll grow into trees,
Swaying in the cool, fresh breeze.

John Ryan Jones (10) Abercraf CP School

THE DINOSAUR

The dinosaurs are dead and gone
Completely disappeared
And no one knows why they've gone
It's very very weird.

Some people say they lost their eggs
Some people say they froze
But the fact is
No one really knows.

When they slept they snored
When they woke they roared
When they walked they stamped their feet
And when they talked they ranted.

They used to live in a cave
They used to live in some water
They used to live on land and sea
But destined not to live forever.

Claire Parsons (9) Abercraf CP School

THE DANCING FLOWERS

I saw them dancing in the sunshine golden,
Their silky leaves have summer in,
Their stalks are the April green grass,
The melody is the wind that blows.

I saw them in the sunshine golden,
Happiness fills the depressed world,
The grass is waving but with no rhythm,
The sparkling sun dies down.

I sometimes watch them dancing,
Upon the hills in Wales,
And when I try to dance like them,
I know I always fail.

Now my poem is at an end,
Do not ask for more my friend,
Very busy I shall be,
Watching the flowers dance in the breeze.

Katie Berney (10) Abercraf CP School

COMPUTERS

My mega drive is a lot of fun,
If it is raining and there is no sun,
Move around with the joystick,
Make your character punch and kick.

Fly on a carpet fly on a rocket,
Buy one to fit in your pocket,
Put the disk in - switch the music on,
Then enjoy the music by the CD-ROM,
Type out a poem type out a letter,
But a drawing is much better.

I would play it all day,
If there was a way,
Yeah my computer's great,
But I tell you what,
Going out beats the lot.

Daniel Roberts (10) Abercraf CP School

THE STARS

The stars like diamonds twinkle in the sky
They shine so very bright
But when the darkness fades away
The stars begin to die.

There are different kinds of stars to see
Southern Cross and Hercules
Some are big some are small
Some you can't even see at all.

I often watch the stars above
I like the Great Bear
But the Little Bear I really love
I'd love to go up there.

Do you watch the stars at night?
They brighten up the sky
I hate it when daylight comes
Because they begin to die.

Ceri Anne Rapado (11) Abercraf CP School

THE WAR ONCE AGAIN

The war is not what you call a lovely thing
When I wake up in the morning,
I hear the thud thud thud of the bombs going off

Thud thud thud
There go the soldiers with their big black boots

Thud thud thud
Pitter patter pitter patter
There goes the metal helmet that's
Not what you call a helmet that's
What you call a cauliflower hat.

Thud thud thud
I hate that sound it is so
Horrible the bombs are bad enough

Claire Kelton (10) Brynhafren CP School

SCHOOL DINNERS

When we go to the hall for dinner,
I put them to the test.
But I sit by a pest,
We sit at a desk,
They are the best.
Semolina is the worst,
It reminds me of something horrid,
I smells like some dirty socks,
Some people like it,
But then again some people don't!
Chocolate crispies are lovely.
When I eat them,
I just want more,
When there are seconds,
There's a line, ten miles long,
Chips are nice and soft,
I like them a lot.
Our cook called Dot likes them a lot,
So does everyone else like them a lot,
Custard is soft and runny,
You can fling it anywhere,
But you wouldn't want to waste it,
I don't want to paste it,
Fling it at the boys,
Yes! That's all right

Julie Burmingham (11) Brynhafren CP School

SILENCE

The chilling silence of a winter's night,
The frost gathering over the soft grass in the field,
Ice building on the pond making a thin crisp layer,
Not a sound from the roosting birds,
Only the eerie call of an owl.

The frost marching over the fields like a little army,
Marching, marching,
Like a land lost to earth,
This landscape shows no time,
An unreal world lost in darkness.

As dawn breaks,
The silence is broken by the lowing of cows in the field,
Like the first creatures known to earth,
Their breath making wisps of steam in the air.

Michael Rickard (10) Brynhafren CP School

THE WAR

I hated the war.
Every time the Britons were eating food my mouth watered.
I could see it there in my mind.
We hardly have anything.
We have to get our own water.
Most of the water we get is dirty.
One child died about every 2 seconds.
We were always frightened.
Being evacuated was horrible.
You had to meet new friends and get used to the way of life.
We were always frightened that it was us that was going to die.
It seems as if it was never going to end.
The bombing was terrible.
It only stopped in the night.
It started in the day again.

Emma Killoran (8) Brynhafren CP School

SCHOOL BLUNDERS

Wake up in the morning,
Get my uniform on,
Open the gate then wait for the bus,
My shirt's hanging out, hair's a mess.

When we get to school I explore for a bit,
Go to walk to school,
But Cruncher the bully beat me there,
I'd better hurry up or he'll catch me like a snare.

Maths first,
Up to the third block,
Sums today the swots say, 'Hooray!'
I knew everyone,
Not!

Chemistry next,
While I am waiting for teacher I made an atomic cocktail,
Everyone tries a bit then starts to grow a tail!

To the lunch-room we go,
Steamed cabbage,
Not as good as my last school!

Games is after lunch,
We play rugby,
I get hit in the chest,
Then I am laughed at by the other players.

So on the first day I turned people into foxes and got my sums wrong,
I wonder what I'll do tomorrow?

Alex Bourne (11) Brynhafren CP School

THE SUMMER

Summer.
Summer is about having fun,
And being happy.
Summer is about going on holiday.
In the summer I like to go to the sea.

I like lots of things about summer,
I like the golden sun,
The golden sun glistening in the blue sky,
The lovely green grass standing on the ground.
In the summer we play in paddling pools
The summer water whirl and still,
You can play with your friends,
You can see the colourful flowers.
In the background you can hear the birds
Out comes the sun,
Now we can have fun.

No more school.
It is way too cool.
No more trees without leaves.

Gemma Jones (10) Brynhafren CP School

HITLER BITES BACK

The war is not a very good thing,
Not a very spectacular thing.
It's when Hitler bites back.

The war is a disaster,
Four million and more Jews dead,
This is when Hitler bites back.

We declare war,
Not a good thing to do.
Sirens to signal the Germans,
This is when Hitler bites back.

The war eventually finishes,
Many of population dead.
We will never forget the day,
When Hitler fought back.

Luke Foskett (10) Brynhafren CP School

WHEN I GROW UP

When I grow up,
I am going to be a hairdresser,
Or a barrister in fact.
That's what I'll be when I grow up.

When I grow up,
I am going to be a horse doctor,
Or a poet in fact.
That's what I'll be when I grow up.

When I grow up,
I am going to be a librarian,
Or a chemist in fact.
That's what I'll be when I grow up.

When I grow up,
I am going to be a vet,
Or headmaster in fact.
That's what I'll be when I grow up.

Or should I just wait instead?

Sian Lloyd (10) Brynhafren CP School

SPRING HAS COME

Spring has come,
Spring has come,
The winter is past,
Buds on trees again,
Flowers have popped out,
All over again.

Spring has come,
Spring has come,
Lambs are born,
Birds are singing their songs again,
Hedgerows are green instead of black,
Aren't we glad spring has come.

Spring has come,
Spring has come,
No more winter,
No more snow,
Aren't we glad winter's gone.

Spring has come,
Spring has come,
Trees are starting to go green,
All over again.

James Wynne (10) Brynhafren CP School

THE MONSTER CALLED MRS MIME

First day in school not enjoying it a bit.
Got a teacher who is horrid cruel and a twit.
'Little girl, little girl,' she says to me, 'Do you think
Spain is next to Hungary?'

Now this is where the bad bit comes into the story.
Maybe a bit disgusting maybe a bit gory.
Came up to me like a bull on fire
tripped over a rather large piece of wire.
So teacher went flying into Peter who I'm
afraid was eating his dinner and his head
got knocked into a jam tart.

Can't wait to get home from the teacher.
I think someone needs to teach her.
She's a monster in disguise.
You can tell she's a nasty one in her eyes.
Thank goodness it's home-time.
Away from that monster called Mrs Mime.

Rebecca Lashbrook (9) Brynhafren CP School

PENGUIN CRAZY

My teacher's penguin crazy,
He likes them very much,
I think he thinks we're lazy.
He would rather teach penguins according to us.

My teacher's penguin crazy
He's a bit of a loony,
My teacher's penguin crazy.
He's losing control.

My teacher's penguin crazy
I can't help that,
He is hazy in the head
No-one can help that.

My teacher's penguin crazy
That's all I have to say,
My teacher's penguin crazy
He's always been that way!

Sarah Vaughan (10) Brynhafren CP School

SUMMER IS HERE

In summer I like going to the sea
My mum, dad, brothers and me
I enjoy swimming in the pool
It makes me nice and cool

All the colourful flowers pop out
I hear a scream and a shout
The birds are singing
The phone is ringing
Oh what a noisy place it is.

Out comes the sun
It's so much fun
There's no more school
Under the tree it is nice and cool.

I'm lying in the sun
Everybody's having fun
All this happiness
Is coming to an end

It's too bad
I'm so sad
It's gone till next year.

Joanne Emberton (9) Brynhafren CP School

MY FRIEND

My friend is very kind,
She makes me laugh when I am sad,
She is fun to be with,
I am glad she is my friend.

We run about together,
She says I'm funny,
But I don't think that,
I can't imagine what it would
Be like without her.

We visit each other's houses,
That is rather fun,
When it is playtime,
We talk till playground is full,
I'm glad we are friends,
She is the nicest person
I've had as my friend.

Christina Maddox (10) Brynhafren CP School

AT WAR

The soldiers start to retreat,
Taking notice of their sweaty feet,
Because day after day they march,
And march,
All they did was stand and wait,
Using themselves as some sort of bait,
Hearing the barking of a machine gun,
Saying to each other 'Who's next?'
All they hear is exploding bombs,
All they see is cut off tongues
All of them are targets,
Shadows, soon to be wiped out,
Trying to forget those times,
Thinking of the future,
And to make new rhymes,
Being happy,
Lucky to have survived.

Timothy Lashbrook (11) Brynhafren CP School

IN SPRING

When it comes spring the birds start to sing,
Then all the bees come out.
The trees grow their leaves
And the grass grows long.
In the house everyone is spring cleaning,
And putting away the hot-water bottles,
Some people are going on holiday to Spain and France.
New baby animals are being born,
Like baby sheep, pigs, cows and horses.
The flowers are coming out on trees
They are also coming out in the grass.
Children are playing in the garden,
The sun stays out later at night.
When you wake up in the morning it is very light
And the birds are singing merrily.
People are doing some gardening,
Like cutting the lawn and pulling up weeds.
Insects are flying around,
They come into the house,
Wasps and bees are building their nests.
I like spring best of all.

Susan Jones (11) Brynhafren CP School

GREEDY HITLER

The war is on
Panic scares come from everywhere
Bombs are splashing
Houses also dashing

Quickly, go into the shelter where it will be safe
Sirens singing
Firemen's bells ringing

All to blame is Adolf Hitler,
Spoiled, silly, also greedy
Trying to take over the world
But I don't think he did, that's what we were told

Soldiers, boys, men, all went off
All the women did all the other stuff
Soldiers fighting for their lives
Soldiers fighting or to die

War has finished
It is all over
But people remembered
What the soldiers have died for.

Sarah Morris (10) Brynhafren CP School

MY FRIEND AND I

When I go to play with my friend we get up to mischief
We scare ourselves stiff
We talk about what happens at school and at home
We talk about burying my mum's best comb
We go for a walk
We ride on a bike
We go for a picnic
We eat what we like
Mum takes us to town
To see a clown
Then we all frown
He's wearing all brown
Then we go home
It's time for bed
Until tomorrow we'll sleep instead.

Sarah Wilde (9) Brynhafren CP School

ME AND MY RABBIT

I love my rabbit, care for it too,
The coat is soft, gorgeous too.
The only problem is I cannot hold rabbits.
My brother always laughs at me.
My rabbit is called Gemima
Sometimes I call her Gemimababy.
I love my rabbit
Sometimes I have dreams about her.
Sometimes I have bad dreams about her.
That she's died.
I feed her, hold her sometimes.
I see rabbits in the field through my window.
My rabbit is brown, it's in a hutch outside.
It loves carrots cut up.
When my rabbit's hurt I am worried about it.
People call me a worrier.
I wanted a rabbit, a brown one, and I got one
but I wanted a smaller one.
But I'm lucky that I've got one.
And I love her.

Laura Brain (8) Brynhafren CP School

SPRINGTIME

I can smell the flowers,
Hear the leaves rustling,
How I look forward to spring.
I see all the colourful flowers,
All the bluebells shoot up again,
Spring is fun,
Spring is exciting,
The nights get shorter,
The days get longer,
I hear the birds chirping,
I see the blue skies,
The tulips open up,
The daffodils start to die off,
The hedges start to grow again,
The lambs are starting to be born.

Charlotte Francis (8) Brynhafren CP School

THE OLD MAN

He's always sitting in a chair,
and his favourite fruit is a pear.

He wanders around the town shops,
yet he always wears green socks.

His house is in a tremendous mess,
and he's even said he's seen the lochness.

He's got a plain brown straw hat,
and he's got an unusual breed of cat.

Jamie Davies (11) Guilsfield CP School

PAST TIME CHILD (VICTORIA SUDDS)

Behind that plain and sturdy face,
lies a feeble, weak, scared girl.
The squint in her eyes tells she's wicked,
confident and positive,
but through her unhappy strong look says
cold and remote against anyone else.
Passing someone in the street tells her to
look down or to give a rude stare.
But with a father like hers who blames her.
A slothful and indolent father who cares
nothing for either of his children (he is carefree).
Now Victoria Sudds lies dead
killed by war, now loved by other men,
for no-one loved this weak, scared girl.
So she ventured to live in another world.

Gemma Lewis (11) Guilsfield CP School

HE'S RICH BUT SO POOR

There's a man who lived Next-door,
Who's rich but so poor.
When he comes home he has no one to meet him by the door
No wife, no child, no son, no daughter I think he oughta.
He has one dog who's blind,
And he feeds him on old bacon rinds.
I went to his house yesterday, but I didn't know quite what to say!
The man got real mad
And that made me feel sad
For the man who's rich but so poor.

Claire Williams (11) Guilsfield CP School

PICASSO THE UNBELIEVABLE

His artistic talent
And his grey, spiky hair,
His angry face with dark staring eyes,
All mixed in one to make one whole picture.

His picture's unbelievable,
He wanted to paint like a child,
His Dad's dream come true,
Paris was his art school.

For a couple of years,
Until he left,
Born in Espana,
Died in France,
Travelled a bit, didn't he?

Didn't become famous
Until his late years,
His hobby, well a womanizer,
With a capital W and N.

His paintings explain it all,
Some finished,
Some unfinished,
But who cares,
He's who he is.

Kate Watkins (11) Guilsfield CP School

WHO'S THAT MAN?

I was walking in the town with Mum when, a man came along with his head down and no smile upon his face.
'Who's that man?'
I asked Mum, 'He looks so glum.'
Mum answered, 'I'm not really sure.'

I went to school the next day, all my pals ran up to me.
'Did you see him again?', 'Who?' I said, 'The man who's always glum.'
'Yes I did, but I still don't know why he's so glum, but I will find out.'

'I saw him again Mum, I saw him again.'
'Who?' 'The man,' 'Oh,' said Mum, realising what I was talking about.
'Mum I want to know what's the matter with him,' I said.
'the only way you are going to find what's the matter with him, is to ask.'

It was Saturday again and I was walking in town.
I saw the man and then I remembered what Mum had told me.
I ran over to the man a little scared.

'What's the matter? You look so glum,' I asked the man.
He didn't say anything.
'Please tell me.' Eventually he said something,
'You wouldn't like to know,' 'I do, maybe I can help,' I said.
'Well,' tears came into his eyes, 'well, my family and house got demolished in World War 2.' ' Oh no, I'm so sorry,' I said with tears coming to my eyes.'
I saw the man running across the street, 'Hey come back.'
He'd gone but someday I'll make him happy.

Lucy Kneale (11) Guilsfield CP School

OLD MAN

Why do you sit alone on the jetty old Mr Jerimiah?
Oh, I don't know, I like to think of the time when I was a sailor.
Tell me some of the experiences you had when you were a sailor.
Then sit down and rest my friend.
When I was a lad of your age I first went on a
boat, I loved the sea and I've loved it ever since.

Lauren Jenkins (11) Guilsfield CP School

STREET PEOPLE

My life is abysmal, I have calluses and cuts,
I live in the gutter with puss and snot.
My house is a box I found on a skip,
My life is with rats and I don't get much kip.
My blankets are bags I found outside Tesco's
With a dustbag for a pillow, I am described as weeping willow.
My sorrows have drowned inside beer that I buy when I have the
Money then I take a long, long sigh.

I am not an ordinary guy, I am not a guy,
I am a low life scum as other people have led me to believe.
But I am keen to learn and eventually teach my colleagues the way of
the sleaze with their cars and no scars.
I am strong inside and I hope to own a string of bars if I have time
before my terminal breath.

Life is the end of existence for me on the back streets, the pavements.
Not even a cave is available to me.
I have no friends of human breed just the vermin which crawl up my
sleeve nipping and biting me giving me rabies, a disease that does not
frighten me. For I am at home with pestilence and three other things
of the apocalypse.
Some day the four horsemen will come and get me, and you, and all.

Jonathan Boshell (11) Guilsfield CP School

THE PAIN OF LIFE

That old man from the market
Stands in solitude in the corner,
Begging for money and for food.
Neglect has taken its toll on his face,
Wrinkles under and around his eyes
A pimple on his nose and his neck
Stiffened by being curled up in a box.

Yes a box (his home)
Filled with newspaper.
Life is of no purpose to him.
His life is in tatters
Not a wife no children
He has lost all contact with the rest
Of his family
Not knowing if they're dead or alive
Why go on? It's the pain of life.

Chris Downes (11) Guilsfield CP School

MY SISTER

My sister is always in my
bedroom.
The little horror wants
to play.
My sister is always getting me
into trouble.
The horror is always stealing my
clothes.
My little sister is always on
my bike.
She is a horror!

Rachel Hamer (11) Guilsfield CP School

THE OLD MAN FROM POOLE

The old man from Poole,
People say he's a fool,
I feel sorry for the old man from Poole.

He is so poor,
And ill from the war,
That poor old man from Poole.

He lives on the streets,
Steals and then eats,
And that's the old man from Poole.

James Griffiths (11) Guilsfield CP School

NEIGHBOURS

Mr and Mrs Naggy going to fish,
this is because it's their favourite dish.
Playing ball, shoo go away,
damn, I knew this was going to happen today.

Their silly hats make them look old,
maybe underneath they are quite bold.
Whatever we do we get told off,
they even comment on how we cough.

Their only family lives in Liverpool,
I feel sorry for them because their gran is quite cruel.
For tea they have black pudding and potatoes,
they aren't very fat but they sure like to pose!

Emma Bebb (11) Guilsfield CP School

THE GALA PERFORMANCE

She stood there,
The tension mounting,
The conductor lifted his baton,
She lifted her violin, and looked at the conductor,
Then she waited.

The orchestra started,
There was a pause.
Up came her bow
And the music poured out,
Like ink from a pen.
And we absorbed it,
As a sponge does with water.
You could hear her.
The soloist.
Her music coming out more victorious
And more beautiful than anything I'd ever known,
Or heard.
Then suddenly, with three last notes,
It was over, just like that.
As if the whole orchestra was to go on,
Playing and playing and playing . . .

Sian Grieve (11) Guilsfield CP School

GHOST!

His voice was quiet and low,
His eyes were dark and piercing,
His life was strange and secret,
I found him so intriguing.

His existence is hardly known,
Among many people around.
For he does not talk to anyone,
And seldom out is he found.

No-one lets his time go by
Time means nothing to him
Time is life and life is time
Because he is lacking in kin.

I cannot find out what is wrong about him,
Yet I know there's something that is.
I have just a small suspicious thought
That something is amiss.

Nuala Ryan (11) Guilsfield CP School

ADVENTURE SHOP

Mrs Davies had owned the shop for five years,
And when it came to money she had no fears.
'I'm a pillar of society, well known and true,
My furniture showroom will completely furnish you.'
Stephanie and Susan were shop assistants by trade,
Polite, pleasant and kind, but both un-married maids.
Blue was their colour, for blouses, jackets and skirts,
Grey for Mrs Davies, such a hurtful colour for a shirt.
Susan was 30 and Stephanie 25, glad to be alive.
Mrs Davies was a septuagenarian, to be exact, seventy-five.

The furniture showroom was packed stocked and full
Locals and visitors had shopped there and still came to pull
The large brass handles on the doorway that lead into the room.
Susan and Stephanie the shop assistants with a smile,
Their customers and delivery men came from both town and miles
Away in the countryside where farmers' farms had been furnished.
But Mrs Davies hid herself away in the office, dimly grey burnished.
The telephone was her favourite object,
'Hello, it's Kathryn Davies here, from the town's jet set.'

Clare Jones (11) Guilsfield CP School

BOB HOSKINS

Bob is always on telly
I think it might have been his ambition for many years!
It has partly come true.
On telly he always seems to have a cheerful smile
but does he always have one at home!
I wonder what casual clothes he likes to wear?
Jeans and a T-shirt, shorts and a jumper or maybe
a shirt, who knows, because I don't.

What books does he like reading:
War books, soppy books, Catherine Cookson, again
who am I to know.

Has he an occupation maybe he is a part-
time policeman, fireman, traffic warden, a nurse,
or a life-guard at a swimming pool
I don't know what occupation he has;
because for all I know he might
just live on TV wages.

The only way to find out all these
things is to ask him or write to him.

Kirsty Edwards (11) Guilsfield CP School

NANNY SANKEY

Nanny Sankey is the best,
She never says that we're a pest
Nan snores all night to her heart's
content, not surprised the money
she spent.

In the war she was a land girl,
Never heard of a pearl,
She's very lucky to escape,
With the chances she would take.

Her and Grandad met at last,
And when a few years went past,
They had five children the boy
Finally came, and Grandad was
not in shame.

Esther Harrison (11) Guilsfield CP School

THE REPEAT OF LIFE

The clock strikes 7.00 and up he gets,
Ready to lay the shovels out.
Twirling his moustache with his finger takes
a lot of trouble and skill.

The clock strikes 8.00 and no customers yet.
Down comes his son and starts to wreck the shop.
'Don't do that my son' he muffled
in his deep and croaky voice.
'What is this strange object here?'
'Electricity, Father.'
'It is an omen. It has got
something coming from it
and it's going into the wall.'

The clock strikes 5.00 and the repeat
of the twirling of the moustache starts.
Collecting of the shovels ends the day for him!

Amy Jones (11) Guilsfield CP School

PEACE

The world could be such a peaceful
place,
If people weren't so bad,
No more crying or bloodshed,
No more children who are sad,
I think we are so lucky
We don't have to shed our tears,
Over fathers dying or mothers
saying
'These are unhappy years'.

Robyn Silcock (10) Llangattock Church In Wales School

PEACE

Peace is a tree covered in white blossoms,
Whenever a soldier dies a flower falls off.
Six years of war and the tree has nearly died,
Its silky petals make a snow carpet on the
orchard floor.
Whenever a bomb is dropped the tree shudders,
A tiny root breaks.

The war has ended.
The tree makes new roots again,
It's covered in blossoms.
A flower is left remembering the dead ones.

Elinor Giles (10) Llangattock Church In Wales School

PEACE

Like pain and agony
And lots of hate
fighting for freedom.
The only thing that keeps them going
Is hope, hope for the future
When all is over
The good defeats the bad,
Once again
The sky clears.
Not all is lost
Then all look up
And see a white dove
Soar up to the sky.

Benjamin Morgan (11) Llangattock Church In Wales School

MEMORIES

A cold graveyard on a gloomy night,
Full of soldiers' graves,
It makes me think of war-time,
Gunshots, bombing and deaths.
But then I think of nowadays,
Peace and peace alone,
Civilisation, friendship,
Love is all around.

Jennifer Marshall (11) Llangattock Church In Wales School

THE SPIDER IN THE BATH

There's a spider in the bath with me
he's floating on the top
If you want to wash
look for something a bit posh
This is wrong for a spider to live in the bath.

I hate spiders in my bath,
I'll shout I'll scream jump and run out.
I won't be in the bath today or, any day.

Jane Gardner (10) Maesyrhandir CP School

EAGLE

Massive wing span
Powerful talons
Scaly claws
Sharp like razor blades
A hooked beak
It is the king of the birds
It lives on rocky cliff's banks
Fast mover
They eat a grouse or a
Rabbit.
Large eyes
Hunter or poacher
Caged up
Shot in the head
Now it can't lay its eggs.

Lloyd Lewis (10) Maesyrhandir CP School

MR RAT

I know little Mr Rat.
He lives under a door mat.
I met him on a rainy day
and I didn't know what to say.
So I ran into the hall
and I began to call.
Mum didn't hear
So I went 'Oh dear.'

So I went to the door mat
and began to call Mr Rat.
Mr Rat came out at last
and this time I didn't gasp.
I said 'Do you want to play.'
He said 'Another day.'
Next day I came again
and I said 'Do you want to play a game?'
First we had a game of Snap
then we had a little nap.

Salome Williams (10) Maesyrhandir CP School

ROBIN

Robin robin you've got a red tummy
You've got a brown back
You play in the snow
You fly in the sky
But nest in the tree
Feed your babies
And eat seeds

Lee Jones (10) Maesyrhandir CP School

EVACUEES

The day was here I was sad,
My mum said Hitler made her mad,
Upset anxious this is how I'll be,
Crying children all around me.

Excited as the train rolled in,
Oh Hitler you have made a sin,
Mothers singing that they are,
The children worried going afar.

Jamie McNamee (11) Maesyrhandir CP School

THE OWL

The owl has a sharp beak
just like the eagle.

The owl has a golden buff
His wise big eyes that glow in the
dark.

Gliding above the green green
field what's that I see down
in the field?
It's a little mouse I see.

He hovers around like a long lost bird
He glides through the air looking
for his prey.

Steven Jones (9) Maesyrhandir CP School

THE PUFFIN

A puffin eats it's its only
wish,
up in a tree, as free as
can be,
his beak is so pointed
it's also jointed,

Up in the rainforest
above the canopy blue,
the puffin flies gently
above you.

Stacey Lovell (10) Maesyrhandir CP School

WHAT IS THE SUN

It is a yellow
football kicked up in
the air.

The sun is an orange
marble that rolls around.

It is a doughnut
covered in lemon curd,
The sun is a round pizza
with extra cheese.

The sun is a lollipop without
a stick, it is a scoop
of ice-cream without
a cone.

Daniel Evison (7) Maesyrhandir CP School

THE GOLDEN EAGLE

A golden eagle is the king of the birds.
It eats mice, foxes and sheep
It nests in cliffs away from people
With its pointed beak it looks very fierce
It could pierce anybody's ear
It is as rare as a peregrine.

Stephen Parrotte (9) Maesyrhandir CP School

SNAKE

The sharp eyed snake with the
scaly skin
lots of people are scared of him.
It slithers about in the green
green grass hissing and squirming
gungy and stretchy.
It's smooth and stripy sticky
and slimy.
He lives under ground and puts
animals in his pound.
For supper, dinner, even tea.
Its teeth are long just like
itself and sharp just like
its wealth.
The shine in its eye is like
a beam.
In fact it's enough to make you
scream.

Andrew Thomas (10) Maesyrhandir CP School

COMMON KESTREL

The common kestrel has
a beak like an eagle,
it's as fast as a leopard,
his wings spread out like
the sun rises. In all
the bird competitions he
will win all of the prizes,
he is as strong as a bear.

Cole Meakin (10) Maesyrhandir CP School

HARRY THE MOLE

Harry the mole is big black.
And pink on the nose.
He's got very small toes.
He sleeps in the mud.
Curled up like a spud.

Leighton Blayney (8) Maesyrhandir CP School

THE BLACKBIRD

The blackbird has black feathers.
Blackbirds have orange beaks.
Most of the blackbirds have brown feet.
All of the blackbirds have yellow eyes.
The blackbirds have black or grey tails
and sharp big grey claws.

Jenny Moseley (9) Maesyrhandir CP School

WHAT IS THE SUN?

The sun is a star
That is hot and gives us
Light.
The sun is a hat
That the clouds wear.

The sun is a yellow eye
That looks down on us.

It is an orange Frisbee
That flies through the sky.

Samantha Watkins (8) Maesyrhandir CP School

GOLDEN EAGLE

The eagle's by the moor today
chasing thrushes by the day
speeding through forests woods and
towns chasing the birds going his
way.

He's as fast as a cheetah
and as fierce as a lion
it's tawny brown like the bark
on a tree
he is as free as the wind.

Ben Lawson (9) Maesyrhandir CP School

OTTER

Otter, otter swimming around.
Under the water you can always be
found.
For fish you're looking.
You use your claws for hooking.
You're brown
You're white
You're silky
You've even got an oily coat.
The people throwing rocks at the
otter he lets out a wail and swims
away.
You're looking for frogs.
Under the logs.
You flop you hop
You flippety flop.
In your holt you're walking around.
There's no need to hide you will
still be found.
You eat insects,
slugs,
even slimy worms.
You're burrowing now I can see.
You're out looking for food for your
babies.
Because you need some new.

You're wet
You're slidy

Katie Jones (9) Maesyrhandir CP School

PARROT

Red, orange, blue, white,
purple yellow with a bit
of green.
Parrot is like a rainbow.
Long feathers long wing
Long beaks.
They live in South America.
They sit in branches.
They speak like humans
They fly
They lay eggs in nests
Parrots make funny noises.
Some live in large flocks.

Alison Evans (10) Maesyrhandir CP School

THE ROBIN

Your colours are orange, brown, white.
Dark black eyes.
Your feet are dark as the night.
The brown tail falls.
Your black beak is small.
You eat seeds and berries.
You have a red breast.
The crown is brown.
You are a seed eater.
Robin flies in the sky.

Gwyneth Lloyd (9) Maesyrhandir CP School

TAWNY OWL

Tu-whit tu-whoo said the owl at night
hunting for fat mice, voles
Owl has finished hunting
Then he carries on with his nest
and he is white brown and grey
He sleeps in the day and hunts at
night. He has a soft fur.
The owl came back out at night
to get some food

Jemma Tisdale (9) Maesyrhandir CP School

BARN OWL

Barn owl barn owl in a big big barn.
He is very calm.
He's so fluffy
and your head is puffy.
You fly in the night
and sleep in the day
you are so scary
Owls love mice
and have a sharp beak.
And sharp claws
and bright eyes
you are so wise
and so big.

Jonathan England (9) Maesyrhandir CP School

ALAN ALBATROSS

Alan albatross is a bird
it doesn't have a cage.
But if you do upset it,
it will get into a rage.
Albatross how big you are
your wings are 8 feet wide.
I hope when I am in trouble
you will be right by my side.
Albatross oh albatross how
very brave you are
McCleach is coming after you
you better fly far.

Daniel Morris (9) Maesyrhandir CP School

MUM

Mum I've dropped Thomas' milk bottle
Well go and clear it up
Mum the wardrobe fell over.
Well go and clear it up
Mum I've dropped Daddy's tool box
Well go and clear it up.
Mum I opened the toy cupboard and all
the toys fell out.
Well go and clear it up.
Mum I've cleared everything up
Well go and . . . oh good.

Sarah Williams (9) Maesyrhandir CP School

THE CHIPMUNK

Chipmunk, chipmunk under the ground
in a hole you can be found.
I can see you scuttling across the
field with your mouth full of nuts
tightly sealed.
Little pink chipmunks asleep in
burrow mother feeds with care a fox
comes along and gives a stare.
But mother chipmunk gives a glare and
the wary fox goes.
You're soft,
you're striped,
you're yellow,
you're grey,
black and white.
You bring seeds and berries to your
young as their lives have just begun.
Again the wary fox comes back for
food but the babies are not there.
So chipmunk chipmunk under the ground
in a hole you can be found.

Emily Fennah (9) Maesyrhandir CP School

EVACUATION

Unhappy they were to leave their families
Upset, angry, worried to go
They were surprised to know that they had to go

Sad disappointed they wanted to come back
to their families
Afraid to come back in case of more bombs
Scared and cross to go to new families.

Kelly Mitchell (11) Maesyrhandir CP School

FOX

Orange brown and black in colour.
Fast sneaky and a pest,
that's a fennec fox that's my guess.
Black and brown scarred head
fed his mate and found some bread.
Orange brown and black again
baggy-eyed, nocturnal, furry tail,
dog-eyed and dog-eared.
It's a cub again.
Golden, brown, nuisance and a pest
baggy coat, tall long ears.
Have you guessed?
Desert fox of course.

David Lane (10) Maesyrhandir CP School

SAMMY THE SNAIL

Sammy the snail,
as slow as a snake,
Sammy the snail,
lives down by the lake.

Sammy the snail,
leaves a trail,
with his house,
upon his back.

Emma Smith (11) Maesyrhandir CP School

FLY FLY

Fly fly you fly so high
Like the birds in the sky,
Oh very high.

Fly fly do not go by
The big spider,
He is a very good hider,
You see I don't lie,
Do I?

Gemma Nay (10) Maesyrhandir CP School

HEATHER THE SPIDER

Heather the spider was playing in the wet weather
pouring with rain. She was not very happy Heather wore a
very wet nappy.

She was happy when the rain stopped she got dry
in the very hot sun and her mum told her off for
playing in the rain.

Jessica Hancox (12) Maesyrhandir CP School

GEORGE THE GOLDEN EAGLE

The big bird with the golden head
Big and strong.
Eats birds' eggs also gazelle
Lives in the mountain way up high
Thinks he can touch the sky
Seeing its prey
Shooting down like a bullet calling
Its prey.

James Burton (10) Maesyrhandir CP School

THE BIG CREEPY SPIDER

One day when I was in the bath,
A big spider came, I was really scared.
I started to scream my head off.
I started to move away.
When I got out of the bath,
It was time to get ready for bed.

When I was in bed, I woke up in pain.
I felt a spider on my head.
It was really furry it stuck to my hand,
When I threw it on the ground it crashed
with a big bang.

Katie Bowen (11) Maesyrhandir CP School

A WUZZY WASP STING

A wuzzy wasp sting is like,
sitting on a pin,
I hate those things that
fly,
because one landed in my
eye.

Those black and yellow pests,
in my garden there's a nest,
that night I went to bed,
one stung me
on my head.

Liam Blayney (11) Maesyrhandir CP School

GOODBYE GOODBYE

Sad to say goodbye
I'll be on my way
I was mad
Because Hitler was bad

Mum said bye
Dad said bye
I'll be on my way
For a jolly good ride.

Sara Ellen Jones (11) Maesyrhandir CP School

TIMMY'S POEM

Timmy the tarantula
waits by his web,
when a fly came
along Timmy tensed
his legs.

When Timmy caught
the fly he wrapped
it up in silk,
he boiled it in a
saucepan and
served it up with milk.

Jay Davies (10) Maesyrhandir CP School

JESUS

Jesus is wonderful.
Jesus is good,
Everybody loves him
And they always should.

He was born at Christmas
Everybody knows,
He died at Easter
And then he rose.

He died for me,
He died for you,
And that is what
His love can do.

Even though he's always there
He is with you everywhere.
Now it's time for me to go
Because I've told you all I know.

Maryann Pryce (10) Penygloddfa CP School

WHAT AM I?

I am sometimes zig zag,
I am yellow, I'm red, and orange and blue.
I am dangerous when you are under a
tree.
I sometimes come when it's very hot
and humid.
It is frightening for some people but
not me.
I can start in a storm.

Rachel Williams (8) Presteigne CP School

SNOW

I lie on the ground, soft and white
cold and smooth in the wintry air,

So quiet and gentle
waiting for the children to play in me,

When the children come with their
sledges and sleighs

The noise they make on those
wintry days!

When I melt the children say
oh! Why did the snow go away?

Rebecca Bennett (7) Presteigne CP School

ICE-CREAM

Zoom zoom come to me
Thinking of you makes me
full of glee.
Magnum white with sickly bits
Full of scrumptious heavenly licks
Zig zag with banana and
Strawberry
Licking you makes me
Glowberry
Solero with orange and cream
You make me fall into a dream.

Daniel Evans (9) Presteigne CP School

EPONA

She rides on a blanket of white
Through a golden mist
Hair flows into many colours
Her gentle dance fills the birds with happiness
Creatures hop and flutter at her side
Her gown of silver shines and
Brings the sky to life
The magical stars leave a path of wonder to follow.

Laura Lynch (9) Presteigne CP School

ICE-CREAM

Love of it
Slick in slender cream,
So lovely makes me want to scream.
Greedily scoop into a spoon,
Almost as good as a trip to the moon.

Skip through a fantasy,
Of tastes that describe thee,
Roses entwined cannot compare,
To the wonderful sight that makes me stare.

Hate of it
Sloppy and sickly,
Runny and sticky.
Must 'ave caught the flu,
Just as bad as being locked in the zoo.

Golly golly get to the lav,
The worst nightmare I've ever had.
I'd rather have toothache or even have nits,
Than swallow this terrible thing on a stick!

Kate Fleming (9) Presteigne CP School

ICE-CREAM

A tingle of sweetness
A chocolate heavenliness
A fresh orange bite
A fizzy lemon fright

Banana and strawberry
Tutti-frutti vanilla
Ice-cream, ice-cream
You make me shiver.

Marie Watson (8) Presteigne CP School

EPONA

She glides through the silky clouds
On fluffy chariot
Her delicate creamy dress
Swishing through the air.

If any cruelty is ever seen
To horse or birds
She cracks her whip
And they are gone in a cloud of dust.

She rides a magical white unicorn
With gentle giant wings
Hopping across the sky
A ring of tiny birds
Surround her head.

Harry Copestake (9) Presteigne CP School

ICE-CREAM

One cold snowy day when everyone's dreamy,
I rush out to find the snow is ice-creamy,
Wake up wake up wake up I shout,
Then Mum and Dad start running about.
We feast all day and all night,
By the glittering sky of ice-creamy light.

Angus Smith (9) Presteigne CP School

EPONA

She drifts off into the clouds,
Mounted on a silken white pony.
Her golden hair flies behind
Mingled with birds of beauty.
All that remains is,
The light from her shining eyes.

Anna Court (9) Presteigne CP School

EPONA

Peacefully gliding on cloud-like horses
Flying through myths and fairytales
Ghostly is she
Birds follow in tribes of magic
Holding flowery necklaces in their beaks
She goes

Tom Bennett (9) Presteigne CP School

ICE-CREAM

Mars, Mars, wonderful Mars,
If I eat you you'll take me to the stars.

Zoom, Zoom, marvellous Zoom,
If I eat you I go to the moon.

Calipo, Calipo delicious Calipo,
I wish you were as big as a hippo.

Solero, Solero, fabulous Solero,
If I eat you I'll fall off my chairo.

Tracy Kuegler (9) Presteigne CP School

ELAN

Dams that are old and slippery,
Waters that are vast and blue,
Roam the mid-Wales countryside,
Through the valleys well.

The land that lies around them,
Holds a hidden secret world,
Full of creeping lichens,
Spiky creatures,
Green and curling ferns.

The Cnwch wood is magical,
Protective and so green,
With all its trusting family,
They all can be seen.

Jocelyn Garman (9) Presteigne CP School

ICE-CREAM

Solero Solero you're one of the few
How much I would like to dine on you
You're covered with lovely orange ice
That I have only afforded twice,
Your gleaming white centre packed with ice-cream
Makes me fall into a heavenly dream
Solero Solero you're one of the few
How much I would like to dine on you.

Joe Nethercott (9) Presteigne CP School

THE WORLD

The world is round,
There are many different countries and places.
Everything in the world is something
But I ask myself what is the world?
It is a dome with humans, countries, places and other wonderful things?
It is an adventure someone has not found?
No-one really knows.
Is there a mysterious animal out there that knows,
Waiting for someone to find it?
Someone might have found it but never returned!
I wonder what it could be like?
Might it have three legs and arms?
It might only have one eye!
Have you ever thought you might be that mysterious animal,
Wandering around out there with that secret in your head,
Floating around waiting to be broken.
Would you tell anyone?
I wonder if you would!
Sh Sh Sh Sh Sh Sh Sh

Simon Millichamp (10) Presteigne CP School

EPONA

Swiftly gliding through magical clouds
On her silvery unicorn called Sparkler
With exotic birds as her followers
A silk gown fashioned from leaves and flowers
Gracefully swaying to the tip of the heavens.
She dreamily twirls through the outer unknown
Universe.

Hannah Weiland (8) Presteigne CP School

EPONA

Gleaming in her silvery coat,
Galloping on her horse's back,
Carefully she moves,
Swaying from side to side,
Flowers and feathers, whirl around,
Landing on her as she passes.

Joseph Seyffert (9) Presteigne CP School

EPONA

Galloping on clouds
On her horse
She is ghostly
Light as a feather
Never ceasing
In her journey
To the heavenly places

Martin Price (9) Presteigne CP School

EPONA

Skipping and twirling
Through the woods
Birds follow
As she rides her horse
Her golden hair
Blows in the breeze
And her gown of feathers
Floats

Jessica Lock (9) Presteigne CP School

LOST, LOST, LOST!

'Mum, can't find my uniform!
Mum, can't find my homework,
Do you know where it's gone?
Oh mum, I've just remembered I have
To write a song!'

'Miss, can't find my ruler,
Miss, can't find my book,
Miss, can't find my rubber,
Oh someone please help me look!'

'Sir, can't find my jotter,
Sir, can't find my pen,
Sir, can't find my compass,'
'Hurry up then Ben!'

Rebecca Rogers (10) Presteigne CP School

EPONA

Proudly she rides on a beach of gold,
Birds circle her horn,
Perching now and then
To sing
A child reaches out to touch,
And feels a ghostly softness,
The horse splashes into the sea spray,
Epona disappears,
Leaving the child to weep.

Edward Wilding (9) Presteigne CP School

GETTING AWAY FROM THE RAIN

I like to fly away by plane, to get away
from the awful rain.
It's the only thing that keeps me sane.
I usually end up going to Spain,
in the sun without the awful rain. I have lots
of fun and never any pain.

The sea is blue and very warm.
The swimming pools are big
I spend most of my time in and out of them.

I hate the day when I have to pack
the cases, saying goodbye,
and travelling to the airport.
I have one thing on my mind, when I land
back in Wales all I will see is
Rain! Rain! Rain!

Carrie Tomkins (10) Presteigne CP School

EPONA

As I gallop through the golden clouds
On my magical pony
Of silver and gold
We fly sunwards
Reaching a secret garden
Where the animals live
We play the animals and I
Then sleep.

Andrew Williams (9) Presteigne CP School

TREASURED

I see him faintly, through the rain,
Dancing in the green blue sea,
As I draw nearer he jumps out of the
water,
Like the sun at dawn,
I wade through the shallow water
to meet my friend,
He lowers his massive silky back
With a slip and a slide I hold onto
his gigantic body,
He jumps and off we go,
We glide through a massive coral
reef,
We play a game,
But I slide off and the dolphin wins,
Before I know I'm back on the shore,
The dolphin smiles and so doing,
He *disappears*.

Helen Pope (10) Presteigne CP School

EPONA

Gracefully gliding on a chariot of cloud
Her hair of silk
Her white cloak gently swirling in the wind
Through a silvery sparkling mist
A glowing silver halo upon her head
Birds singing
Fluttering beside her
Braids of hair upon her stallions
She floats away into the distance of unknown.

Oliver J Levick (9) Presteigne CP School

MY PETS

My cat sleeps all day,
In the night she wants to play.
Always with me no-one else
Just me!
In bed she comes and jumps at my head.
But then crash bang bang crash smash
I say get downstairs. Miaow
No go!
I say oh Cherrishnic and she goes.
My rabbit is a very messy pet
He rips up his paper and makes it wet.
And he tips up his food.
I think he is in a bad mood.
My bird Archie nibbles his millet while playing in his cage.
He comes to you and you give him a dandelion then
he eats it with his feet.
My fish swim and hide in the weed because they are scared of
me.
They dash and splash about.

Nicola Bateman (10) Presteigne CP School

EPONA

Birds sang to her
As she journeyed into the flowered forest
Misty clouds descend and surround her
And the flowers grow to meet them
She follows the birdsong
Into the secret world.
Through the entrance flies
A butterfly
All alone so sad
Epona picks her up
And sets her free.

Emma Gore (8) Presteigne CP School

HOLIDAY

I went on holiday down by the sea
The shells and sand were lovely to see
The sea was warm, the stones were cold
The fish swam past in lots of three.

I bought an ice-cream
My sister did too
We sat on the beach and a crab bit my toe
Soon I had to go
So goodbye holiday
See you next year.

Thomas Davies (10) Presteigne CP School

HARVEST TIME

The cockerel crows to wake you up in the
morning time.
To harvest out with the combine harvester
To cut the corn,
To make the bread,
To take to the shop,
To sell to pay for seeds to grow more corn
for bread.

Brian Stapleton (10) Presteigne CP School

MY PETS

Sparky is my puppy,
Ziggy is my cat,
The pup would love to have a game,
But Ziggy just sits and spits.
I do hope they get together
It's up to the pup whether,
He can control his playful ways,
Be faithful friends for the rest of their days.
If the barking doesn't stop,
I guess Ziggy will go over the top!
Sparky has a very sharp tooth,
If he bites Ziggy's fur would hit the roof!
My happiness would be complete,
If from the plate they would eat the meat,
I place before them with great care,
For both of them the love I share.
Leave out barks, miaows and bites,
Become sweet loving mites,
Then I can leave them at home all day,
Knowing they will gently play,
Guess this is a dream,
'Cos cats and dogs do not team!

Rachel Blythin (10) Presteigne CP School

MIXED DAYS

Rainy days are awful
Rainy days are bad
Rainy days make me sad

Sunny days are good
Sunny days are hot
Sunny days make me happy

Windy days are cold
Windy days are wild
Windy days make me mad

Alex Griffiths (10) Presteigne CP School

CAMPING

I'm going to camp with my
friend for two nights,
Out in a big green tent,
I'll be able to run and shout
without anyone saying be
quiet all day.

I will sleep in my new sleeping bag,
I will wear those jogging bottoms
that I had from great auntie May
the green and blue ones with
the *big* grass stain.

I can get dirty as much as I like,
I can make mud pies and keep
them all the time I stay.
My friend is like me so he will
agree maybe he's got something
lined up for me.

Sarah Owens (10) Presteigne CP School

SUMMER'S HERE

Summer's here
The grass is green
The birds are singing their hearts out
With joy.
People going on holiday
At the seaside.
Building sandcastles,
Paddling or swimming in the sea
Laughing with joy.

David Price (9) Presteigne CP School

HEART BREAKS

My heart is broken,
    No more love
    No more happiness,
    Just sadness,
But wait here she comes,
    Her sweet eyes,
    Her sweet scent
        is mine again,
            at last.

William Bufton (10) Presteigne CP School

IN THE NIGHT

Lurking slowly through the night,
In the mysterious forest of shadows.
The creeping predator spies its victim.
A scream, a flash of light,
'Are you alright?'
'I heard you scream.'
'It's OK Mum, it was only a dream!'

Jemma Owens (10) Presteigne CP School

RAINY DAYS

It was a rainy day
And I couldn't go out to play
People jumping in the puddles
Splish splash getting wet again
Standing inside the door getting changed
I said to my mum can I go out to play?
But mum said back to me 'Ten minutes
because it's nearly time for tea.'
'Mum can I go out after tea again please?'
'Yes OK then but try to keep clean.'
'I didn't get dirty I stayed nice
and clean just for you.'
The next day I went out it was
raining once again
I put on my wellies and my rain coat too
I went out to play on this rainy day
I splashed in all the puddles
I played football with my mates
But this time I got muddy and
had to come in and change
My mum got cross and grounded me
Now I'm not allowed out on a
rainy day.

Robert Davies (10) Presteigne CP School

MY FAMILY

My dad's a country bobby,
His number's 806,
Always there to lend a hand
To people in a fix.

My mum works at the Post Office,
Selling papers, cards and sweets.
And when we go to meet her
She often buys us treats.

I have an older brother,
He's up, just like the lark,
To the paper shop, six days a week;
Goes by the name of Mark.

My little sister, she's called Jess,
She's only five years old;
She's very caring with other kids,
And usually good as gold.

And me? Well, Man United is my team,
I have a friend called Carrie,
And if you haven't guessed by now
My name - of course - is Barry!

Barry Davies (9) Presteigne CP School

SPIDERS

Spiders work away spinning their golden webs.
But in the morning when a fly goes
trespassing it gets stuck -
Then a spider sucks his blood
and that's the end of a fly!

Jason Creemer (10) Presteigne CP School

THE FARM

The cockerel crows to wake us up
Today we are off to bale.
Scratched legs and aching backs
And lots and lots of hay stacks.

Lambs skipping in the field
Cows grazing by
Tractor pulling heavy load
Soon be home for tea.

Joel Layton (9) Presteigne CP School

MY FAMILY

Mum busy as a bee,
Dad upstairs as calm as can be;
Melissa drinking a cup of tea said
'It's *horrible*' gave it to me.

Peter begging for walkies,
Grandad telling Nanna porkies,
Auntie Linda's getting slim,
Uncle Brian's beard's trim.

Karen, Graham, cousins too on a day
trip to the zoo.
That's what they do!

Francesca Withnell (10) Presteigne CP School

MY DIARY

I have a little diary
I lock it up tight
I write up all my secrets
In it at night.
When I get tired
All I have to do
Is turn off the light
And have a nice snooze.

Angharad Matthews (9) Presteigne CP School

THE SWIMMING GALA

One more race and then it's my turn,
Must try hard, can't go slow,
Come on Presteigne, make more haste,
We haven't any time to waste,
All silent waiting for the whistle to blow,
My team shouts out, go Hannah go.
The water rushes past my ears,
Soon I lose all my fears,
The silver bar I see ahead,
Oh *no* I'm beaten by a thread.

Hannah Deakins (10) Presteigne CP School

THE TYPICAL HOUSEKEEPER

Miss Feather was a bony old woman, she
applied for a job at our house.
'Sorry' she said 'the meat's a bit cold,
and the gravy is lumpy and don't feed
the dog.
The Yorkshire puddings were hollow and
burnt,
I fed the carrots to the rabbit,
the peas are a bit shrivelled up.'
'Has everyone finished?' Dad asked
'Nobody has started' I replied . . .
Everybody scowled at the thought of
seconds.
She announced that pudding wouldn't
be long
'What is it?' my sister said
'Well um' she shivered 'Crumble'
'What type?' She dropped it on our
white carpet.
'Tomato' she sniffled and walked out
of the front door. 'I could not
live with her cooking' Dad said as
he walked towards the cooker.

Megan Griffin (10) Presteigne CP School

THE WIND

As I walked through the woods in the night,
I heard the wind, the wailing wind.
As I heard the wailing wind,
The ghastly, ghostly wailing wind,
I shivered.

Dewi Evans (11) Ysgol Gymraeg Ynysgedwyn

WIND

No-one knows what I am,

No-one knows where I go,
But I whistle down your chimney,
And I bang at your door.

I'm blowing round your country,
I'm blowing down your street,
And when you're on your bike,
I'm blowing at your feet.

I mess up your flowers,
In your back yard,
And when you go to parties,
I blow away your card.

Adam James (11) Ysgol Gymraeg Ynysgedwyn

THE WIND

As I walked through the misty woods,
I heard the wind hover above me.
The branches of the trees were swaying,
Swaying in the whistling of the wind.

I walked deeper into the woods,
With the wind blowing behind me,
Dangerously it came bulging at me,
Shivering and frightened I ran.

Suddenly it stopped,
The swaying of the trees stopped too,
There was no whistling to be heard
Nobody knows where it went,
I wondered, while I stood in the misty woods,
All alone.

Rhys Morgan (11) Ysgol Gymraeg Ynysgedwyn

THE WINDY WIND

As I walked through the woods,
The strong wind blew towards me,
Dangerous, invisible and cruel,
I screamed as it whistled past my ear.

The wind's a vandal,
It blows down trees,
It blows off roofs on houses,
It's the ghostly vandals of earth.

Hywel Rees (11) Ysgol Gymraeg Ynysgedwyn

WHAT IS THE SEA?

The sea is a dark blue car
Ready to reach the sand.

It is a flying butterfly
Bathing on the shore.

It is a dark blue pencil case
Waiting to close.

It is a paradise beach
About to be soaked.

It is a blueberry sweet
Queuing to be unwrapped.

It is a salty blue tube of glitter
Bursting Open.

James Jones (10) Bedwas Junior School

BONFIRE NIGHT

F lying high
I n the sky.
R ockets
E nchanting the air.

W hizzing wheels
O range and
R ed.
K illing colours
S urfing the sky.

Lucy Rawlins (10) Bedwas Junior School

CARNIVAL NIGHT

The screams and shouts
As the roller-coaster goes round
On carnival night.

The lights flash and the
Bumper cars bang
On carnival night.

The fluffy sweet taste
Of candyfloss melts in my mouth
On carnival night.

The bobbing horses
Of the carousel
On carnival night.

Lights turn off,
Screams disappear
Sleepy feet go home
From carnival night.

Andrew Bate (11) Bedwas Junior School

NIGHT TIME

One dark misty night
An owl was squawking in a tree
A fox walked in the short green grass.
He is looking for his prey.
The stars shine
Next to the moon.

James Fullalove (10) Bedwas Junior School

THE SEA

The sea is a lion,
He lives in a cave.
His mane is the sand,
He feels soft and fluffy.
His prey is a human.
His enemy is pollution.

Matthew Evans (9) Bedwas Junior School

HAPPINESS

Happiness is in my mother's warm face
When she greets me from school on a frosty day.
It is lambs skipping on the mountains,
It is wedding bells on a hot summer's day.
I feel happiness when my 15 cats
Snuggle into my arms.
It is friends dancing around me.
Happiness is Bedwas our village.

Abigail Watts (9) Bedwas Junior School

THE SUN

The sun is a yellow lion
Looking down from the world above.
All the clouds obey him,
He's king of the sky.
At night he rests on fluffy white beds of clouds.
He's red hot,
No-one dares go near him
As he shines bright in the air
Proud of his yellow skin.

Jessica Williams (9) Bedwas Junior School

I STILL REMEMBER

I remember the smells of the different rose trees
In my nan's back garden.
The colours were so pretty,
The smells were so sweet.

I remember the gardens on holidays
Where the squirrels run and bury nuts
Ready for the autumn and winter to come.

I remember Christmas mornings
Peeping out of my bed clothes
To see if Father Christmas had paid a visit.

I remember my rabbit Lucy
With silky black fur
Who died the other day.
But I'll still remember.

Rebecca Morris (11) Bedwas Junior School

ON THE DOORSTEP

Standing on the doorstep,
My heart beating faster and faster,
I heard a big crash,
As dustbin lid fell.

I saw a huge grey shape,
Lurking in the shadows,
I ran down the street,
But the shape followed close.

I lifted my hand,
The shape lifted his,
When I looked closer it was only
My shadow.

Jodie Cantello (11) Bedwas Junior School

THE PIER

Over the gleaming ocean,
The one hundred year old pier appears.
People fishing over the edge,
As children dive for the ice-cream parlour.

Big fish, little fish,
Being caught,
Pulled up on rods.
Dusk dawns and the pier is forgotten,
By most people,
But not me.

Rebecca Evans (11) Bedwas Junior School

FRIENDS NO MORE

No more laughter
No more fun
The clock has stopped
But life goes on.

All we now do is look and stare
And turn our heads in despair.
Both too scared to admit who's wrong
In our hearts our friendship goes on.

All good times we used to have
Are nothing now
But memories.
Friends no more.

Natalie Meredith (10) Bedwas Junior School

ALONE

Alone
Like a pigeon amongst a flock of ducks,
I got lost in a crowd of people.

Scared and frightened,
Terrified, goosebumps,
Shivers down my spine,
Knees knocking like a ticking clock,
Stomach churning like a spinning top.

I felt the darkness surround my thoughts
I heard the speakers call my name.
Then the darkness went away
Until I'm lost another day.

Elizabeth Crane (11) Bedwas Junior School

MY HOUSE IN THE DARK

As I approached the door of my house
        in the black of night
I heard the howl of a dog
        and the crunch of ice
Under my feet as I walked.

I saw the mist tumbling down
        the mountains like waves
Crashing against the rocks at sea.

I turned quickly as I thought
        there was a monster
Behind me, but it was
        only the shadows of a tree.

I smelled the smell of the last
        chimney going out
And the smoke rising into the sky.

I felt scared as I heard
        the scream of a cat.
Then the black sky started to turn purple
        as a ray of light appeared
Behind the mountain.

Shena Neville (11) Bedwas Junior School

FLIES

One day I saw a fly
Who caught my very eye
He gave me a grin
So I splattered him.

Siân Rose (11) Bedwas Junior School

SPOOKY NIGHT

Walking through the village
Darkness falling quickly
Moon shimmering brightly
I hear dogs barking loudly
I smell old smoke from a chimney
I feel the cold around me
Under the full moon.

Hayley Wells (11) Bedwas Junior School

THE CLOUDS

C rashing thunder
L ightning flashing
O ver the seas
U nder the trees
D ashing through the sky, the
S torm is here.

Lois Creed (10) Bedwas Junior School

GAS

Gas is a mosquito,
Flying around in the air,
Waiting for its victim.
It spots a human,
Flutters over to it and bites.
It hovers in the night sky,
Still happy with the blood
That it has sucked.

Tywi Roberts (9) Bedwas Junior School

THE STING

Creepy crawlies crawling around
In the air and on the ground.

Ants scurrying round and round
Picking up things they have found.

Flies flying in the skies
Hitting people in their eyes.

Woodlice climbing in and out of trees
People being stung by ferocious bees.

Lee Simmonds (11) Bedwas Junior School

IN AN AUTUMN MORNING

In an autumn morning
I can see a squirrel scuttling along the branches,
I can hear a rabbit burrowing in the leaves,
I fan find a squirrel nibbling nimbly,
It can smell a dog approaching,
I can see a hedgehog clambering along the flower bed.

Rhys Elsworth (9) Bedwas Junior School

WATER

Water is a giant stamping on the ground.
It lives on top of the cliff.
His long beard shining like silver.
Its hands are as hard as steel.
Its prey is us.
The giant's enemy is man.

Julie Crane (9) Bedwas Junior School

ELECTRICITY

Electricity is a snake
Slithering and jumping.
It stings with its poisonous venom.
Its eyes glow at its hunted prey
As it jumps and kills the helpless.

Stephen North (9) Bedwas Junior School

THROUGH THE WINDOW

I see the grey road
Travelling down Church Street.
I see the green trees
Growing tall outside my home.
I see the gardens
As they bloom with coloured flowers.

Nicola Barker (8) Bedwas Junior School

THE HAND

This is the hand
That shuts the book
That swats a fly
This is the hand
That writes with my right
And does what's left
With my left.

Matthew Bissett (8) Bedwas Junior School

THIS IS THE HAND

This is the hand
That picks the flower
That rides my bike
That carries my bag
That grabs my toys
That paints a picture
That throws the ball
That catches the cat.
This is the hand
That wrote this poem.

Emma Turecek (8) Bedwas Junior School

MY MOTHER

She was . . .
A clever card player,
A coffee drinker,
A fast swimmer,
A tasty cooker,
A hard worker,
A blue and red dress with
A blue shiny ring to match
She is . . . my mother.

Dana Seaborne (8) Bedwas Junior School

WHO AM I?

I am fierce
I live deep in the forest.
When children pass by
I jump out and gobble them up.
I have sharp teeth.
Who am I?

Samuel Williams (8) Bedwas Junior School

WHO AM I?

I am small
I am brown
I wear a red hat
And a blue coat
I am furry
I have got a little red jumper
I am Paddington Bear.

Caroline Hughes (8) Bedwas Junior School

RECIPE FOR AN IRON MAN

Take a big metal box for the body
And thirty crushed grey cars for the legs.
Take a cylinder painted grey for the head
And bolts for the eyes.
Take steel spikes for teeth
And you will have an iron man.

Jennifer Hearne (8) Bedwas Junior School

I CAN

My hands can touch.
My hands can help.
My hands can write a poem.

My eyes can see
The sky, the clouds and sun,
Gardens, motor-bikes and dogs.

My feet can move
Across the floor
And take me to a friend's.

Natasha Turecek (8) Bedwas Junior School

THINGS I CAN DO

I can make shapes
And turn pages of a book.
I can press buttons
And switch on the radio.
I speak to my friends
And say, 'Do you want to play?'
And I can say, 'Please,
Can I stay up late tonight, Mum?'

Laura Murphy (8) Bedwas Junior School

WINTER

Winter comes,
Wrap up warm, and run outside,
The winter snowflakes fall gently onto the ground,
Pick up the snow, it tingles your fingers.

Winter suddenly pounces on the children,
        the air drops in temperature,
There is a sudden chill,
Winter's grip gets tighter,
        waiting for children to submit.

Winter runs on, through the bare forest,
The silhouettes of trees sway in the breeze,
Then unexpectedly winter loses its strength,
        the air gets warmer, the snow melts,
Spring comes.

Owen Burgess (10) Langstone Primary School

THE WATERFALL

Gushing, pushing,
Pouring, roaring,
Curling, whirling
Down it goes.

Rising, leaping,
Darting, parting,
Prancing, glancing and dancing.

Whizzing, hissing,
Waving and raving.
Creeping, sweeping,
This is the waterfall.

Bethan Coole (10) Langstone Primary School

SPACE

Space . . .
The final frontier.
The sun's glare shining over the planets.
The dead silence,
The dead world,
The cold atmosphere,
The unexplored world awaits man.

Space . . .
The final frontier
The stars of Leo and Scorpio sit dead still
in the sky,
Stepping onto the moon,
First step,
First footprint.

Daniel Weston (10) Langstone Primary School

EARTHQUAKE

The ground trembles,
The earth cracks,
The land subsides,
Buildings fall,
The dust flies,
It is as if the earth explodes.

People yell,
Mourn the dead,
Some survive but some not so lucky,
Lines come down,
Power is off.

David Reece (10) Langstone Primary School

MY GRANDMA

My Grandma has blue eyes
and light brown hair.

Late morning I come to see her,
She's still in her dressing gown.

My Grandma makes me laugh,
She's fussy and tidy,
Always late for things.

Every evening she's in the kitchen,
Cooking Grandad's tea.

He sits in his chair,
While he reads the paper.

My Grandma is kind and gentle,
She is tall and slim.

She's got a cat called Jolly.

I think I'm very lucky,
With my Grandma just living along the road
from me.

Some people have to go a
long way to see their grandparents.

My Grandma is so fussy.
Everything must be in its right place.

My grandparents never miss the news.

I love my Grandma.

Lauren Masters (11) Langstone Primary School

I WISH I COULD

I wish I could step in a rocket,
And fly up high into space,
I wish I could walk on the moon,
And see its big, bright face.

I wish I could wear a space suit,
And come face to face with the sun,
I wish I could see some aliens,
Wow! Wouldn't that be fun.

I wish I could float in the air,
And see all the bright, shiny stars,
I wish I could see all the planets,
Like Mercury, Venus and Mars.

I wish I could walk on the moon,
And see its big, bright face,
I wish I could step in a rocket,
And fly up high into space.

Laura Cansfield (11) Langstone Primary School

FRIENDSHIP

Friends,
Dedicated companions
People who are there for you, always.
In times of sadness, distress,
They don't talk
They listen.
You break up,
It shouldn't last.
They will trust you and care for you
Love you and help you.

Friends,
Someone who trusts you,
Goes with you,
Everywhere.
A person who laughs,
Cracks jokes,
Who doesn't laugh for the wrong reasons.
We won't talk over the phone
We will talk in the bedroom,
At night when it's dark
We will calm each other.

Friendship should last,
Not die away.
Friends
For always
Forever.

Katie Farrands (11) Langstone Primary School

THE DEATH OF ATAHUALLPA

Two headed creatures with four
heavy legs,
and huge chomping
teeth
as big as a parrot's
beak.
The emperor
is in the Spaniards' hands,
a deal is made,
7m tall and 7m
long.
Atahuallpa thinks nothing
can
go wrong.
A room full of priceless
treasure.
The leader keeps his word,
The Spaniards do not,
The leader is
betrayed.
Atahuallpa
is dead.
A storm is brewing
ahead,
Thunder *booms* like a big
drum,
and lightning strikes
a mighty spear. The sun is falling,
It has become forever night, (it is a sign)
It is a sign from the gods.

James Bowler (10) Langstone Primary School

HIDE AND SEEK

You can't run,
You can't talk,
All you can do is hide.

You can't breathe,
You can't move,
All you can do is hide.

I wonder where . . .
What's that?
Footsteps!
Oh no!
I wonder who it is?

Is it John?
Is it Jane?
Or is it Mum playing a record again?

Phew!
That was close.
Oh no!
I've caught you!

Well done Jane!
What a good seeker you are!

Helen Price (10) Langstone Primary School

MY VILLAGE AT NIGHT

Sad, scared I feel at night
The street light suddenly, flashes off,
Everything is dead,
Wind is slipping through the trees,
The moon has lit up the sky
All I hear is the muffling of the night,
The sky has darkened,
I'm getting more scared,
In the houses the rooms are dark and
dismal,
All I can hear is a mouse running,
Running, running.

Kate Hobbs (10) Langstone Primary School

JUST IMAGINE

Just imagine skies of green,
And elephants flying through the air.
If there was a land like this,
I would definitely be there.
Just imagine seas of gold,
And fish were talking loud and bold.
Pencils could jump and walk about,
And rubbers could talk and shout!
Books could turn their own pages,
And a minute lasted ages and ages.
Holidays were going to Mars,
And there were supersonic cars!
Just imagine houses that fitted in your pocket,
And cars that came in a locket.
If there was a flying mat,
Just imagine that!

Lyndsey Parry (10) Langstone Primary School

EXECUTION OF ATAHUALLPA

The time for mourning
has come.
Death has come
over this land.
They invaded, betrayed
and executed.

Call themselves
fighters, more like
Brutal murderers.
How dare they!

Peace is the
One most wounded
in this war
of hatred.

Now instead of
drums for the
next praise,
Thunder and lightning
is all to
be heard.

The Spanish are
the fools here.
It's just a
war of greed.

Danielle Darbyshire (10) Langstone Primary School

A TRIP TO JUPITER

As further into space we cruise,
I find myself reeling,
I find it hard to explain,
The way I was feeling

I'm finding space queer,
While we're getting the cameras ready,
As Jupiter draws near,
The ship becomes unsteady.

Storms rage below,
In Hydrogen gas,
As we orbit around slowly,
Investigating this mass.

We leave the spaceship there,
For a short space walk,
The cold we cannot bear,
To the spaceship we return.

Our mission now is over,
Our engine makes a flare,
After all this we are glad,
To return to the media's glare.

James Johnston (10) Langstone Primary School

WHEN LAVA POURED

Like dripping blood,
Boiling hot,
Bubbling over,
Like soup in a pot,

It curdled and hissed,
Like a snake,
In a bush,
Frightening and scary,
To prey on a bird,

But now is all quiet,
The streets,
All alone,
The people have fled,
Some day they'll be back,
And it will happen again.

Aimée Pollard (10) Langstone Primary School

I'M LEFT OUT

Nobody likes me,
It's as if I'm not there,
They just carry on with their own little lives,
It's not fair,
Being left out,
It's a horrible thing,
I desperately wait,
For the bell to ring,
I'm not noticed,
Unless I cry,
And sometimes, just to get attention,
I do try,
But still, never mind,
The show must go on,
I'll just have to get used to,
Spending life on my own.

Susie Squire (10) Langstone Primary School

IT'S MY TURN TO HIDE

It's my turn to hide,
It's my turn to hide,
Oh what fun,
It's my turn to hide.

Where will I go,
The wardrobe, the cupboard,
Or under the bed,
Or what about the chest?
No, I'll hide under dad's
Rover ZX.

So off I went with my doll in my arm,
'Ready or not here I come,' shouted Elizabeth,
Then I heard another voice,
Another voice I knew quite well,
The door opened and out came dad,
Got in his Rover ZX and drove away,
Not knowing I was there,
Poor old me I have to say,
Went up to heaven on that day!

Jody Summers (10) Langstone Primary School

ON THE FARM

A noisy tractor pulling strongly,
While a creeping rat is sneaking quickly.
But a proud gander struts poshly,
And a strong horse is running fast.
Suddenly a blind mole is digging madly,
The waddling duck is swimming cheerfully
With the big cow eating lazily.

Michael Hayward (10) Llantilio Pertholey School

MY FARM

The mucky sty shelters safely,
A proud goose prances fancily.
The white house gleaming and clean,
My grandchildren growing fast,
The tractor ploughing the field.
A wild horse running free.

Gareth Edwards (10) Llantilio Pertholey School

ANIMALS AND THEIR HOMES

A comfy sty shelters safely,
But dirty pig eats messily,
Tired cow mooing gently,
And fast horse trots quickly.
New-born chick waddles proudly,
Big dog barks aggressively,
And bright hay rots slowly,
Lush green fields ready for
animals.

James Wham (10) Llantilio Pertholey School

ON THE FARM

The warm sty covers safely,
Mucky pigs eat greedily,
The comfy hay spreads everywhere,
The noisy mower is cutting grass,
All the old wood is rotting slowly.

Daniel Morgan Maddock (10) Llantilio Pertholey School

OUTDOOR LIFE AT A FARM

The tractor is muck-spreading the field,
Machinery ploughs up the country.
Strong harvester cuts fast,
The barn smells warm and sweet.

Matthew Worgan (10) Llantilio Pertholey School

THE STY

The comfy sty shelters warmly.
Some mucky pigs eat hungrily,
The massive trough is dirty and mucky,
Some smelly slops stink horribly,
A big gate creaks powerfully,
The new wood protects safely,
The soft hay spreads cosily.

Bethan Williams (10) Llantilio Pertholey School

CHAOS

Chaotic, lack of order, running wild,
Completely hyperactive with never-ending creations.
Just so insane and confusing,
And which runs through the human eye.
Mad, dangerous and out of control.
That's what chaos is.

Chaos!

Lewis Morgan (11) Llantilio Pertholey School

FARM ANIMALS

The mucky pig is eating greedily,
A proud goose is prancing fancily,
Noisy dogs are howling restlessly,
While tip-toeing spiders creeping soundlessly,
The gentle cows are chewing quietly,
The safe barn is sheltering and cosy.

Kirsty Hicks (9) Llantilio Pertholey School

THE FARM

The cosy pigs are sleeping soundly,
But the sweet barn is smelling sweetly.
The proud goose is prancing fancily.
Some lovely hay is going quickly.
The milking cow is mooing noisily.
Some coloured fish are swimming splashily,
And the noisy dogs are barking fiercely,
The smelly stable is packed with horses,
The noisy tractor is spreading slowly.

Jessica Collins (9) Llantilio Pertholey School

THE PRANCING GOOSE

The goose is prancing proudly and flapping her wings
A rat is balancing steadily and slowly,
And a horse is jumping over high fences.
A cow is lazing and eating greedily,
The chicken is clucking loudly,
And the house is comfortable, warm and safe.

Matthew Bevan (9) Llantilio Pertholey School

GRAVITY PULLS

Gravity pulling things down that's me
I'm strong so, I can beat you any day
I'm bossy so don't hang around with me
And I'm impatient

So get down . . .

. . . *here.*

Jade Perkins (11) Llantilio Pertholey School

THE BARN

The pig eats messily,
The delicate food tastes charming,
The sweet hay smells luscious,
A warm bed is comfortingly cosy,
The sparkle of webs twinkle in the light,
Spiders running lightly in the beam,
The rotten manure spreading richly,
A comfy barn shelters safely.

Holly Williams (10) Llantilio Pertholey School

PERCY PRESSURE

Percy Pressure is a big fat man,
He likes to wear tight clothes,
He hates it when you pump a balloon,
He hates it when you puff your cheeks,
He hates it when you hold your breath,
He hates it when you eat baked beans,
He hates these things because
he is full of wind.

Rhys Davies (10) Llantilio Pertholey School

FARM ACTIVITIES

The blue jeep is roaring loudly,
But the small spider is spinning quietly,
A horrid rat is scuttling quickly,
And an old tractor is pulling slowly,
The big barn cosily crowded,
With milking cows moving hungrily,
And a small lamb skipping merrily.

Peter Jay (10) Llantilio Pertholey School

ALL ABOUT THE HEART

The Heart is a passionate
Organ,
It beats emotionally,
It helps you feel soft-hearted
tender and tearful,
but when you smoke it's
dying,
and you're killing it away,
'Please don't kill me' said the Heart,
'I want to live another day.'

Bethan Viveash (12) Llantilio Pertholey School

FORCES

The strong forces of pulling
Gravity can pull down.

The impatient pushing of forces
Gravity can pull down.

The desperate children forcing
to jump high. They jump high but
Gravity can pull down.

The great gymnastics jumping
from the rings, they force themselves
up but

Gravity always wins!

Lindsey Woodcock (10) Llantilio Pertholey School

GRAVITY

A cool, smooth, big-headed force,
Who likes to be in control,
Arguing with anything that moves,
He thinks he is important,
But he's really a threatening bully.
His grip is really tight,
And if you try to get free
He'll put up a fight.
He's a business type of force,
Who never has time to play,
But he always brings you down.

Christopher Hill (11) Llantilio Pertholey School

GRAVITY

Gravity a powerful beast,
Commanding, overpowering,
A monstrosity,
Pompous, stuck up and arrogant,
Pulling down planes kept aloft by his
enemy, Air Resistance,
Taking birds out of the sky,
Crumbling even houses and trees
He'll always bring you down.
He unites planets,
He crushes black holes,
The creator of stars, also their
destroyer,
Our universe is his domain.

Josh Wardle (11) Llantilio Pertholey School

PRESSURE

A big, crushing, mad man wanting
        to be top,
Thinking power, might and glory
        Stamping up and down,
Embarrassed by his size and
        Slow moving,
But powerful and deadly.

Boom!

Thomas Varley (11) Llantilio Pertholey School

AUTUMN

When autumn arrives after summer,
Leaves change colour too,
Tanned mahogany, bloodstained scarlet, and pale yellow.
Breezes gently make trees,
Sway from side to side,
Remains of leaves,
Drift down slowly and softly,
Flickering as they fall,
The pearl white frost,
Arrives and kills some plants,
Cowering and creeping,
Frost freshly laid at down,
Over crunchy crispy leaves,
Causing them to rot away.

Donna Norris (10) Llantilio Pertholey School

DAY-DREAM

People call me air resistance,
I'm a very frisky person
lively and energetic,
tossing everything around,
helping everyone in my way.

I'm very light and wispy,
I'm always rushing around,
I'm very very day-dreamy
my head's always up in the clouds.

Stacey Bamber (11) Llantilio Pertholey School

FRANK GRAVITY

He is strong, he'll pull you down
because whatever goes up must come down.
He's a selfish chap and is always arguing but
one thing's for sure he'll never bargain.
He thinks he's the best and he won't
rest until he's won.
Aeroplanes, satellites, helicopters and birds he pulls
each one down to earth.
You can't stop him, he'll pull and pull and slowly
you will come down.

Jonathan Ruck (11) Llantilio Pertholey School

GRAVITY - THE SUPREME POWER

Gravity is strong and masterful,
Bossy and always kingpin,
The centre of the Universe,
Gravity cannot be beaten,
He is always boasting about his mighty strength,
and whatever goes up,
comes straight back D
O
W
N

Anthony Jones (11) Llantilio Pertholey School

AIR RESISTANCE

Air resistance always there helping here and
everywhere,
Air resistance never far helping your kite
to reach a star,
Air resistance never wrong helping planes on
journeys so long,
Air resistance having fun flying planes towards
the sun.

Christopher Thomas (10) Llantilio Pertholey School

CRAFTY GRAVITY

I'm always ahead of other people,
never wait for anyone.
I pull people down to earth,
Bossy, always impatient.
In the end I always get my man.
But this is certainly not the end
Always getting a piece of the action
Very well built, I like to think
Forceful to people to stay down.

Ryan Jones (11) Llantilio Pertholey School

AIR RESISTANCE

I'm so happy, funny and speedy
Thin and wispy darting through the air.
Scatter-brained, smart and brainy
Easily persuaded
I help people fly hang-gliders and kites
I'm a very nice person
Helping people fly high
When I'm done I fly through the sky

Speeding!

Abigail Thomas (11) Llantilio Pertholey School

THE HEART

The heart is red,
Like blood,
Flowing like a river,
It beats,
Sometimes fast and sometimes slow,
When you are broken-hearted,
Your heart breaks,
Your heart doesn't stop,
Only your love has died.

Ellen Beaumont (11) Llantilio Pertholey School

CHAOS

Lights flashing
Music playing
Uproar Riot
People spinning
Feet shifting
Mad Insane
Colours cycling
Crowds moving
Frantic Chaotic
Chaos!

Tom Birkett (11) Llantilio Pertholey School

MACHINES ON THE FARM

The red tractor is dragging,
A noisy muck-spreader shooting muck
The strong manure is smelly and rotting
And the sharp plough turns the earth
Then the seed drill sows the seed.

A bladed mower is cutting the grass,
The spiked haybob turns and heaps.
The clever baler makes the bales
And a special digger piles them high.

Angus Macintosh (9) Llantilio Pertholey School

FARM LIFE

Dirty pig is eating quickly
Comfortable sty shelters him warmly
Creepy spider spins slowly
Noisy horse is neighing loudly
Contented cow has been milked
Cosy barn snuggles warming.

Lucy Niblett (10) Llantilio Pertholey School

CHAOS

Rain is *so* chaotic
never knowing when, where or how
flashing and splashing
like supersonic darts
tap tap *tap*
furiously tapping
It's just complete
anarchy
No rules, no laws
just
Chaos

Kelly Owen (11) Llantilio Pertholey School

FARM MACHINERY

Gigantic combine harvester cutting corn,
Powerful landrover travels all terrain.
Loud tractor pulls trailer,
Sharp baler mows hay.

Filthy muck-spreader spreads the muck.
Strong forklift carries pallets,
Enormous lorry transports potatoes.

Stefan Skinner (10) Llantilio Pertholey School

WHAT IS SPACE?

What is space?
I want to know,
Is it black with deafening silence?
Tell me please what is space.

Is space airless,
With lots of aliens,
Floating around making silly noises?
You can shout as much as you like
Nobody will hear you.

I'd like to know is space a wasteland?
What atmosphere goes on?
I wonder, I wonder,
I'd like to know.

Elizabeth Taylor (10) St Alban's RC Primary School, Pontypool

SNOW

Snow is beautiful
Pretty and clean.
It's white and smooth.
Cold and frozen,
Glistening in the sunlight,
Untouched and unseen,
It sounds like polystyrene,
Squashy underfoot,
Soft and slippery too,
It sparkles on the floor,
Beneath the snow the floor is cold,
On the roof the snow is soft and untrodden.
I love the snow and snowball fights.
I go home and play in the snow with my friends.

Gemma Abramczyk (11) St Alban's RC Primary School, Pontypool

SNOW

Snow is gentle.
Snow is cold.
Your legs are perishing.

When you crunch your feet in the snow it is like polystyrene breaking.
When you look at snow it glitters.

The snow on the roofs is untouched.
When you look out of the window it is breathtaking.
Nobody has stepped on the snow except the birds.

The pond's frozen and slippery,
The snow is as white as white.
The snow is undisturbed.

The snowflake has eight glistening sides.
Snow is like a blanket.

Ben Smith (10) St Alban's RC Primary School, Pontypool

SPACE

The moon is silent,
And shines at night,
It is not a planet but a satellite.
The red planet known as Mars,
Galaxies and shooting stars,
Unknown, suspicious, quiet too,
The deafening silence will get to you.
There's a missing planet so they say,
And galaxies so far away,
Stars, moons, meteors, that's what people say,
Andromeda and the Milky Way.

Stephen Taylor (11) St Alban's RC Primary School, Pontypool

MY FRIEND MORDY

I have a friend, his name is Mordy.
He is as big as my little finger,
And I know because I've seen where he likes to linger;
In my thoughts and dreams
But mainly my imagination.

I have a friend, his name is Mordy.
He really is so cute,
And for his nickname I call him Mini,
Because he is minute.

I have a friend his name is Mordy,
Only I can hear him talk.
When I go running down the street
Only I hear the pattering of tiny feet
As I take him for a walk.

Emily Jordan-Patrikios (10) St Alban's RC Primary School, Pontypool

WAR!

Soldiers everywhere,
Marching bravely down the road,
Their guns held high on their shoulders,
War has begun.

The sirens warn us that bombs are falling.
The race to the bunkers begins.
Huddled together safely while the brave soldiers are fighting.
How many will come marching back guns held high?

Fifty years later the old soldiers are still marching for peace,
Remembering their friends who didn't come back,
There was Victory in Europe once more!

Matthew Dennehy (10) St Alban's RC Primary School, Pontypool

SPACE

Space is filled with a deafening silence.
It has millions of planets which have creatures on
With powers beyond our belief.
The moon is a satellite
reflecting the sun's light on the earth at night.
I hope I am still alive when they explore other
planets,
Because space is a giant wasteland,
Waiting to be explored!

Joseph Gower (11) St Alban's RC Primary School, Pontypool

WAR POEM

Children cry,
Adults die,
Fire spreads,
Bombs are dropped.
The Army comes.
The Navy comes.
People yell and hit.
Hopefully in the end,
Victory and peace will mix.
But even then,
The lame,
The sick,
The blind,
Will still remember it.
Even the ones who didn't suffer,
Will remember the war.
Even the ones who were too young to know,
Weep at the thought of Grampa John or brother Joe,
Who died for their country.

Jasmine Slingsby (10) St Alban's RC Primary School, Pontypool

SNOW

Shattering ice in a cold winter,
People curling up to a fire with hot drinks, it makes you think,
People homeless freezing up,
It shows up our luck,
We lie safe in bed,
but they lie down almost dead.
Snow is a comfort to us,
but to them it's a pain.
We treat it as a game,
Snow is fun, it's soft and cold,
We like snow.
Every time the winter falls,
snow covers all the walls,
We cannot play with footballs
Although we have lots of falls,
We all love snow.

Alexander Roberts (11) St Alban's RC Primary School, Pontypool

WAR

War is bad.
It makes people sad.
I can hear people crying.
People are dying.
Bang goes a bomb!
The fighting goes on and on.

More soldiers in the street.
I can hear marching feet.
Bang! goes another gun.
I must run!

Sirens are going.
It's awful knowing
My family could die.
It makes me cry.

Jenna Lear (10) St Alban's RC Primary School, Pontypool

SNOW

Snow is spotless,
Snow is pure white,
Little birds play in it,
Snow is beautiful,
Snow you can have fun with but it can be dangerous sometimes,
Snow is fantastic,
I love snow,
Snow is pretty,
Snow is icy,
Snow is crunchy,
I love snow,
Snow is smooth,
Snow is lush,
Snow is glittering,
Snow is sparkling,
Snowflakes are not all the same,
I love snow,
Snow is nice,
Snow is slippery,
I love snow.

Carol Carey (11) St Alban's RC Primary School, Pontypool

A CHIMNEY BOY

Up the chimney I go again
While sweat drips down my aching head.
The more I go up the hotter it gets,
The smoke comes down from the chimney ahead.

I'm gasping for breath,
It's hard to breathe,
It's dark and grim,
God cleanses my sin.

Danielle Watkins (10) St Gabriel's Primary School, Ringland

BLAZING CHIMNEY

Blazing fire burning hot
        Slipping down
            down
             I
             go
Sweating, and sooty
tired and hungry.
When can I go
My hands are aching
gasping for breath

What a hard day's
        Work

Natalie Moreland (11) St Gabriel's Primary School, Ringland

THE CHIMNEY BOY AT WORK

Tick tock tick tock my clock goes once again.
Another tiring day at work is
just about to begin.
Up a stuffy hot chimney pot.
The soot goes in my eyes.
A roasting fire is down below.

I'm hungry and thirsty
I need a rest
The sweat keeps dripping on
my chest.
I reach the top of the chimney pot
I know I'm there
One more step
I'm out of breath.

Sarah Nolan (10) St Gabriel's Primary School, Ringland

CHIMNEY SWEEP

Victorians were very poor and cruel.
I would sweep all day in any
House.
I would get five shillings a
Week to feed the family.
I would work all day with
Cuts and bruises.
I would be scared and hungry.
One day I nearly broke my
neck but broke my leg
Instead.

Marc Gunn (11) St Gabriel's Primary School, Ringland

AS IT WAS LIKE, AS A CHIMNEY SWEEP

One day at home I lay on my bed,
A knock at the door shook my head,
I raced down to see, but I only cried,
My father had sold me to a chimney sweep,
A shilling a week for working so hard,
I once cleaned a chimney, a dirty piece of brick,
As sooty as can be, but I finally got it clean with
a bit of bother from my master all day,
All he said was 'Work you little brat or you'll get
no pay.'

Leon Trezise (11) St Gabriel's Primary School, Ringland

A CHIMNEY SWEEP

A chimney sweep
climbs dark damp chimneys
cold, hungry with an aching head
I'm suffocating and lonesome
tired and trapped.
When I go to sleep, I sleep in
sooty dirty clothes.
Being a chimney sweep
it feels like nobody cares.

Esther Gush (10) St Gabriel's Primary School, Ringland

LONELY CHIMNEY

Unhappy moments of sooty surroundings.
Cold damp smoky chimney.
Sadly missing my family at home who
sold me for a shilling.
Scared and tired hungry and wet.
Hoping I was some place where I could
be loved,
    and
        never
            be
                lonely!

Katie Rudge (11) St Gabriel's Primary School, Ringland

CHIMNEY GIRL

Sold for a shilling,
I felt cold,
Scared,
Lonesome,
Sneezing from coal,
Crying for hunger,
I sleep in the soot,
I'm on my own
No-one can help,
I can't wait to get home.

Haley Fraser (10) St Gabriel's Primary School, Ringland

A LONELY PLACE

Crying for help
No help came until
I yelped.
I was sad, cold and hungry
But no-one came.
I was stuck,
Up there alone.
But I can't go home.

Nadia Llewellyn (10) St Gabriel's Primary School, Ringland

A NIGHTMARE FOR CLIMBING BOYS

Climbing boys climb dark damp places,
Where the soot hides their faces.
With their sacks on their backs,
Will they ever come back,
Poor old chimney boys.

Screaming 'I'm choking'
Man thinks I'm joking.
I feel sick, will he give me a kick,
Poor old chimney boys.

Amy Prothero (11) St Gabriel's Primary School, Ringland

A HORRID JOB

Climbing boys had horrid jobs
Trapped in chimneys long and thin
Knees and elbows scraped
But they didn't cry
In dust and soot they'd work all day
At night they'd pray that one day they
would get away.

Helen Corten (11) St Gabriel's Primary School, Ringland

VE DAY POEM

Again I can see the light
Shining now so bright
No more sirens
No more bombs
Just people singing joyful songs.

Decorations in the air
For everyone to share.
Eating bits of food
in a joyful happy mood.

And now no more people crying
No more people dying
No more evacuations
Just everyone enjoying
the special occasion.

Nicola Scarpato (10) St Michael's School, Newport

VE DAY

It was the 8th on a music day
No siren sounds,
or bombs dropping.
All were walking with
excitement and jubilation.
I can see the remaining
buildings standing high
and tall.

The view was amazing
loud bangs,
But not guns or shells
Just party poppers in the
street.
And it was a delight
to see the light.

The feeling was emotional
all around the street.
For all who won't
come home.
There were changes
too.
No more ridiculous Anderson
shelters
Now windows with a view,
Daylight shines through.

Karl Johansson (10) St Michael's School, Newport

THE WAR IS ENDED - IT'S SO SPLENDID

People clapping, singing
Happy as can be.
Smelling happiness
in the air.
Mum and Dad singing
like mad.
Jolly old men dancing
like they're two.
The war is ended, it's
so splendid.

Food and drink
to enjoy.
The evacuees coming
back to see their mummy.
Children running and
jumping like monkeys.
The war is ended, it's
so splendid.

No more bombs or
gas masks.
Just happiness
all round.
The war is ended, it's
so splendid.

Louis Yendle (10) St Michael's School, Newport

THE GHOST OF THE MARIGOLD

It was a dark and misty night
As I looked out over the sea.
I shivered as I watched the waves,
Splashing against the lonely quay.

Then I thought I glimpsed a ship,
Gliding through the pitch black waves.
It headed for a big black cliff,
Then disappeared into some caves.

I ran along the harbour top,
Not noticing the cold.
Looked down the cliff and saw below,
The wreck of the Marigold.

And then before my very eyes,
A ship arose, a flash of light,
A ghostly crew moved round the ship,
Which sailed away into the night.

Clare Hutchinson (11) Thornwell Primary School

ALL ALONE IN MY HOME

Here I sit all alone
All alone in my home
Waiting for the phone to ring
Or anything to help bring
Happiness to me

Is that the postman that I see?
Bringing a letter addressed to me.
Oh, alas it's not to be.
He's dropping it at number three.
So I'm alone, all alone . . .

Hannah Sterry (11) Thornwell Primary School

THE SCARECROW

I have ragged gloves
A hat full of hay
I have old clothes
I stand all day
I'm as lonely as can be
Standing up straight
The birds nest on me
I'm nothing but bait
I've only one leg
Made out of wood
It is a peg
Oh! I wish that I could
Lay in the sun
And be like you
Now that would be fun!

Louise Skidmore (11) Thornwell Primary School

INFORMATION

We hope you have enjoyed reading this book - and that you will continue to enjoy it in the coming years.

If you like reading and writing poetry drop us a line, or give us a call, and we'll send you a free information pack.

Write to

Young Writers Information
1-2 Wainman Road
Woodston
Peterborough
PE2 7BU